ILLUMINATIONS.COM

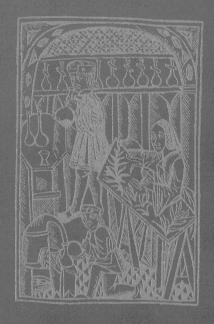

THE ANCIENT AND HEALING ART OF AROMATHERAPY

ILLUMINATIONS®

THE ANCIENT AND
HEALING ART OF AROMATHERAPY

CLARE HILL

Ulysses Press

Published exclusively for ILLUMINATIONS.COM
by Ulysses Press, P.O. Box 3440, Berkeley, CA 94703

ISBN 1-56975-234-6

First published in Great Britain in 1997 by Hamlyn, an imprint of Octopus Publishing Group Limited

Printed in Hong Kong

WARNING: Essential oils should be used with care. Always refer to the Warning which appears on page 39 of this book before using any of the oils. This book has been written and published strictly for informational purposes, and in no way should be used as a substitute for consultation with your medical doctor or other health care professional. All facts in this book came from medical files, clinical journals, scientific publications, personal interviews, published trade books, self-published material by experts, magazine articles, and the personal-practice experiences of the authorities quoted or sources cited. You should not consider educational material herein to be the practice of medicine or to replace consultation with a physician or other medical practitioner. The author and publisher are providing you with information in this work so that you can have the knowledge and can choose, at your own risk, to act on that knowledge. The author and publisher also urge all readers to be aware of their health status and to consult health professionals before beginning any health program, including changes in dietary habits.

Contents

Introduction

Throughout the ages, plants have been used for their mysterious healing properties. Many ancient cultures believed they contained magical remedies to cure the body, enhance the mind and repel bad spirits. But, despite the fact that the therapeutic benefits of plants have been known for many, many centuries, the last two decades have seen a tremendous resurgence of interest in our ability to harness these benefits through the essential oils the plants yield.

While plant constituents are to be found in abundance in modern-day medicine, there is an overwhelming interest in using plants in their most natural forms. Aromatherapy does just this. By capturing the essence of the oil from various different parts of the plant their beautiful, healing and mood-altering characteristics can be unleashed to improve the mind, body and spirit.

The Perfumer's Costume,
Nicolas de Larmessin (c. 1695) ▶

The History of Aromatherapy

Ever since man first began to record history, there are references to the use of precious essential oils to honour, seduce or delight the rich and powerful. It is thought that their use goes back as far as 7000BC, when Neolithic man combined olive and sesame oils with plant fragrances to produce ointments. The use of oils is documented in some of the earliest Chinese writings, and numerous excavations of artifacts produced by the Greeks, Romans and Persians show that they all embraced the power of mysterious, pungent and mood-enhancing plant essences.

Ancient Egyptians

Papyrus manuscripts record that during the reign of the Egyptian pharaoh Khufu, the Great Pyramid builder who lived c. 2700BC, temple incense and other perfumes, fragrant herbs and oils were valued highly and the latter were key ingredients in the healing salves that were used.

In their quest to ensure that the afterlife was as comfortable for their kings and queens as their Earth-bound lives had been, the ancient Egyptians entombed them with precious objects. These included urns containing fragrant oils, prized for their health-giving properties. When King Tutankhamun's tomb was opened 3000 years after his death, the calcite pots with which he was buried still gave off a faint fragrance of spices such as frankincense when opened.

Sennufer wearing perfume bottles, Egyptian mural (1580–1340 BC) ▶

The embalming process to ensure the royal corpses were preserved for the afterlife used numerous oils with fragrant, antiseptic and antibacterial properties. To mummify the corpses bandages were steeped in oil essences of frankincense, myrrh, clove, cinnamon, cedarwood, cypress and spikenard, as well as numerous other oils and spices.

Many wall paintings of ancient Egyptian tombs show the importance of aromatic oils in the daily lives of the court. One mural depicts lively dancers and musicians wearing scented cones on their heads. As their body temperature rose during the performance, the cones would gradually melt and drip their pungent aromas over their hair and body. Others show slaves pressing the oils and many contain figures bearing the precious unguents in amphorae or urns.

Of the many fragrances used in these times, kyphi was one of the most popular. Its name means 'Welcome to the gods' and it was burned in the sun god Ra's honour every day at Heliopolis, the City of the Sun, as the sun set. Kyphi was viewed as some kind of 'wonder drug' – it comprised over 16 different essences and was used as a sleeping aid, as a dream-enhancer, as a stress relaxant and also as a treatment for such diverse ills as asthma and sorrow.

Such was the conviction that the ancient Egyptians had in plant essences that Cleopatra strewed her room knee-deep in rose petals to capture the heart of Mark Anthony, believing that when the petals were crushed underfoot the devastating aphrodisiac properties of the oil contained within the petals would be unleashed.

Many of the temples had separate rooms for the preparation of sweet-smelling offerings to the gods. In the Temple of Edfou, a room was uncovered during excavations which revealed detailed formulae inscribed on the walls for the many different perfumes the pharaoh and his family required. The statues of the gods were also covered in precious oils.

Nebamun's wife wearing a scented cone on her
◀ *head, Egyptian mural (c. 1500–1295 BC)*

Ancient Greeks and Romans

The ancient Greeks had only one word – *aromata* – to describe all the various aromatic spices, medicines, perfumes and incense they used widely. The priestesses at Delphi used burning bay leaves to induce a trance-like state which enabled them to foretell the future, while the handsome, virile athletes at the ancient Olympic games anointed their bodies with scented oils before competing.

But not all Greeks were in favour of the use of aromatic oils. Socrates took a dim view of perfumes, believing that they would blur the distinct boundaries that existed between free men and slaves, as the latter would be able to mask the smell of their sweat which so clearly announced their rank in life.

Ancient Romans, too, honoured the use of fragrant oils and those who could afford to bathed in perfume. Bathing was an important ritual to the Romans and, as a race devoted to sybaritic activities, aromatic oils and unguents played an important role in stimulating their senses and enhancing their physical well-being. During the reign of Julius Caesar communal bathing was always followed by a massage of sweet-smelling oils which were then scraped off the body using a special tool.

The sense of smell was highly valued and exploited by the Romans. When guests arrived to see the Emperor Nero he had them sprayed with particular oils to put them in the mood of his choice. Many of the festivals and ceremonies beloved of the Romans involved great expenditure on scent-providing materials. Perfume was sprinkled on the spectators at games and petals were strewn before men of rank so that they could walk on a bed of sweetly scented flowers.

Young girl filling a perfume bottle, Roman mural
◀ *(c. 2nd century BC)*

肺系

九節

六葉在前

兩耳在後

The East

While the inventor of the art of distilling plants to extract their pungent oils is still disputed, the Persian philosopher and physician Avicenna, born in AD980, is certainly credited with improving the technique. He wrote a book, *The Canon of Medicinae,* outlining the methods used, which was deemed a standard 'handbook' for many centuries. Avicenna was a great advocate of massage, believing that it produced 'repose' by dispersing unwanted matter within the muscles which were not removed by exercise. The massage, performed with oil or perfumed ointments, was, he claimed, an efficient way to banish toxins within the body and eliminate fatigue.

In the Bible, too, there are many references to oils. When a sinner – some say it was Mary Magdalen – first met Jesus, she washed his feet with her tears, dried them with her hair and then anointed them with a fragrant oil she carried in an alabaster urn.

Virgin and Child with Mary Magdalen
and St Catherine, Rafaellino (c. 1479–1527) ▶

Ancient Britain

Having made the connection between mood-enhancing aromas and the power of religion, the Ancient Britons, particularly the Druids, favoured herbs that induced mind-altering states to enhance their mystical experiences. The druidic priests and priestesses burned their offerings during ceremonial worship of their gods, during magical rites and for the 'miraculous' healing of the sick.

Many of the causes of sickness were attributed to evil spirits entering an unsuspecting person and hence exorcism was the only cure. The smoking out of these evil spirits with powerful aromatic herbs was widely used. Juniper, particularly, was linked with purification and was thought to be at its most effective during the winter solstice when the sun died and was then reborn.

This inheritance survived the dying out of the Druidic faith and was widely used by Celtic folk. The tradition lived on and as each invading nation swarmed across Ancient Britain, they brought their own remedies with them which gradually became incorporated into common use. Much of the knowledge of plants and their healing properties was cultivated by the monks who grew the herbs they needed to fulfil one of their major tasks – caring for the sick. They tended their monastery gardens and grew a wide range of medicinal plants. As they travelled to various other monasteries, they swapped advice and knowledge, as well as seeds and cuttings from the plants.

With the arrival of the Normans, the custom of strewing floors with aromatic leaves became common, as it was believed, quite rightly, that the antibacterial properties would help ward off disease and deter fleas and lice. It also reduced the stench of unplumbed housing and ameliorated the fact that bathing was considered unhealthy, if not positively dangerous.

Middle Ages

The crusading knights of the Middle Ages learned from the Arabs the arts of distillation which led to the setting up of apothecary guilds. The spices and oils required by these guilds were imported at great expense using trade connections with the East and, together with the indigenous herbal medicines which had been used in Northern Europe since time immemorial, they were absorbed into the healing arts.

The Knights Templar and the Knights of St John were travelling monks and hospitaller orders. When they returned from the East after the Crusades they brought back new plants and plant remedies.

In the 14th century a devastating bubonic plague spread throughout Europe, destroying more than a third of the population. Fleas living on migrating rats were believed to be the cause. Physicians treating the afflicted wore protective clothing filled with various spices, including cinnamon and cloves. They also carried pomanders studded with cloves and hung garlic around their necks to protect themselves against contracting the dreaded disease. They may well have succeeded, as garlic, cinnamon and cloves are today renowned for their antibacterial, antiviral and antiseptic properties. Interestingly, above all other professional groups, the perfumers are said to have had the highest survival rates during this time. This is attributed to their close proximity to the healing plants and oils.

Breviary of Henry I of Este,
illuminated manuscript (c. 1500) ◀

Man on his horse with his wife riding pillion,
illuminated Book of Hours (c. 1500)

The Renaissance and Beyond

During the 15th and 16th centuries perfumers widened their art, putting plant essences to darker uses. It was said that Catherine de' Medici included her perfumer in her retinue as a precaution against intrigue when she moved to France to marry the king. Her perfumer was skilled in the art of making lethally poisoned – but very fragrant – gloves which she then dispatched to her enemies.

During this time, many great herbalists whose writings drew on experience and experimentation rather than on myth and folklore came to the fore. Mayster John Gardener wrote about the healing powers of plants and their essences in his book *The Feate of Gardening*, published in 1440; Dr William Turner, Dean of Wells and also known as the Father of Botany, published his *New Herball* in 1551; John Parkinson, the apothecary of James I, wrote his *Theatrum Botanicum* in 1640; and in 1653 William Culpeper, probably the most famous herbalist of them all, wrote his great tome *The English Physician Enlarged*, or the *Herbal*, which formed the basis of all subsequent herbalism in the English-speaking world.

Elizabeth I was, like her countrymen, very fond of perfumes and had her clothes, gloves, cloaks and shoes all heavily doused in various different aromas. Louis XIV of France was also a great user of perfumes and insisted that his courtiers wore a different perfume each day of the week to suit his varying moods.

By the end of the 18th century and the beginning of the 19th century the use of oils and perfumes as medicinal products had declined, as more had become known about synthetic drugs. Oils and essences were relegated to the minor realms of scented toilet waters which were sold for the smell alone, not for any therapeutic, healing, mystic, aphrodisiac or ritualistic purposes.

Portrait of Queen Elizabeth, The Pelican Portrait,
Nicholas Hilliard (1547–1699) ▶

Modern Day

However, the powers of plant oils and essences were not to be neglected for too long. Rene Gattefossé, often referred to as the father of modern aromatherapy, first coined the term 'aromatherapy' in the 1920s while studying the powers and properties of essential oils. He thought that although the oils were externally applied, they were able to penetrate to the organs because the skin is interrelated with the brain and nervous system. He believed that the nose and the skin could conduct the beneficial effects of the oils to the relevant parts of the body. His work was put to the test when one day in his laboratory he accidentally burned his hand. Plunging it into a container of pure lavender to cool down the burn, Gattefossé was to discover that the burn quickly lost its redness and swiftly began to heal.

Jean Valnet, a Parisian medical doctor, discovered Gattefossé's research and began experimenting with essential oils and recording his results. In tandem with his work, Madame Marguerite Maury, an Austrian, also studied the penetrative abilities of essential oils, basing her work on Gattefossé's research and working in collaboration with her husband, who was a practising homoeopath.

Gradually, we have come back to the beginning, and have the same appreciation of the potency of smell as when the ancients used their oils for their strange, mysterious rites. Today, though, we have science to reinforce many of the findings of the ancients. Whether you believe all that is claimed for the oils is your choice. The powers of many of the oils have been scientifically backed up by research, while others only have the attribution of many, many skilled practitioners. But all that really matters is how you react to the oils. Over 4000 years of using essential oils indicates that we, like the ancients, are just as susceptible to the seductive powers of smell.

Parfum, magazine illustration,
Jane Harding (1914) ▶

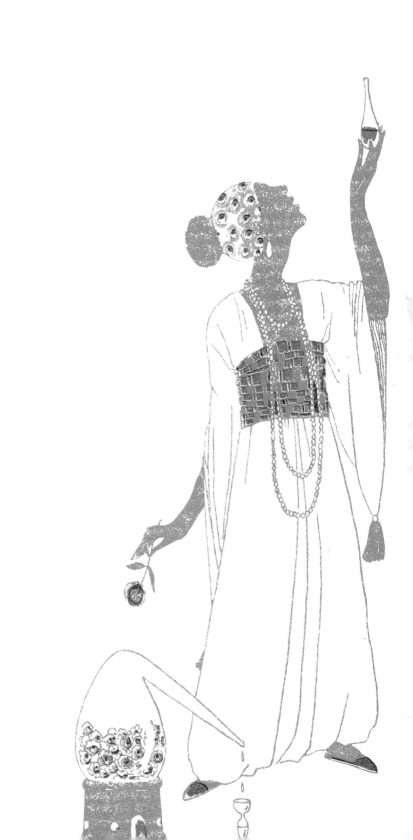

Making Essential Oils

The precious drops of essential oils, which carry so much potency and power, can perhaps be described as the captured vital life-essence of the aromatic plants. These essences are extracted from different parts of the plant – the leaves, flowers, roots, berries, fruits, sap, stalks and stems.

The plants are sourced, as they have always been, from all four corners of the world – jasmine from Morocco, sandalwood from Mysore, frankincense from Africa, geranium from Egypt, Russia and China, ginger from the West Indies and patchouli from Indonesia. Each culture has used the plants for many, many generations and as knowledge of their powers spread so, too, did the distribution of their essential oils.

   Each oil given up by the plant has its own unique aroma, with the ability to affect both the mind and body. Although we can harness the value of the essential oils for our use, it is thought that the plants produce the oils for their survival. The oils help to attract bees and other insects for pollination, to repel predators and to act as hormone regulators by influencing development and controlling the health of the plants.

Illuminated world map (c. 1480) ▶

Harvesting the plants

The art of obtaining the oils is quite complex. Harvesting the plant at the right time to extract its oil is critical. As the concentration of oil in the plant is at its peak during warm weather it must usually be harvested then. It must also be picked during its normal 'awake' state. For example if, like the jasmine, it produces its scent at night, it should be picked at that time. Ylang-ylang flowers should be picked early in the morning, as this is when the perfume is at its strongest. Coriander oil has to be extracted when the fruit is ripe but pepper oil must be obtained before the berries begin to ripen. Age is also important. The jasmine must be picked on its first day of flowering, while the sandalwood cannot be extracted until the tree is at least 30 years old and at least 9m/30ft high.

As with all crops, the quality of the harvest is dependent on whether or not the weather was kind, the soil was properly fed and the pest infestations were warded off efficiently. This means that, like wine, there are good and bad years for the essential oils. As also with wines, the best quality essential oils tend to be the most expensive.

Each species contains a different amount of oil, those which bear the least oil usually being the most expensive. For example, it takes 100kg/220lb of rose petals to extract just 50–80ml/1¾–2¾fl oz of essential oil. Lavender, on the other hand, has more oil glands in the plant and so is cheaper than rose oil. Lavender will produce almost 3 litres/5 pints of essential oil per 100g/3½oz.

Extracting the oils

Although good-quality essential oils are expensive to buy, almost all need to be diluted in a carrier oil or in water before they are used and usually only 2 or 3 drops are required. The potent oils are extracted by using one of the following methods.

Distillation

Distillation is used for plants whose properties are not damaged by heat and is the method used by the ancients. This involves steeping the plant parts in water and then heating them until steam containing the essential oil is produced. The more modern and most common method is to put the plant parts into a still and feed high-pressure steam into it. The steam absorbs the essential oil and is then cooled so that the water and oil separate.

Expression

Expression is used to extract the oils from the peel of citrus plants such as lemon, orange and lime. The peel is pressed over sponges which absorb the oils and are later squeezed to remove the essences.

Enfleurage

Enfleurage uses the flowerheads of the plant which are placed in layers over a fatty substance such as lard, wax or suet, although sometimes olive oil is used. The petals are replaced every few days until the grease is saturated with the essence. It is then washed with alcohol to obtain the extracts. Any essence remaining within the grease is used for making soap. Enfleurage is a lengthy process and so is normally used for flowers such as neroli, rose or jasmine where the oil would be destroyed by other methods.

Maceration

Maceration requires soaking the flowers in a heated oil until the petals soften and their cellular structure releases the oils.

Solvent extraction

Solvent extraction is a more complex method and uses volatile solvents such as petroleum ether. The plant parts are put into a vat with the solvent until they are saturated with the essential oil. The solvent is then filtered to remove the oil.

Perfume manufacture in Nice, magazine illustration (1863)

Using Essential Oils

The oils exert their unique properties by influencing both physical and emotional states. Although skin is impervious and water cannot penetrate it, its upper layers can hold moisture for a short time – this is what happens when we lie in the bath too long and our fingertips become wrinkled. However, provided that their molecular structure is very small, the skin can absorb some substances and these include essential oils.

The physical effects of the oils

It is thought that the essential oils are absorbed by the skin through the tiny hair follicles covering the body. The oil joins and mixes with the sebum at the base of each follicle and then diffuses into the bloodstream or is carried by the lymphatic system or the intestinal fluids.

When massaged into the skin the oil stimulates the circulation and gets the blood pumping around the body more effectively, allowing the oil to exert its pain-relieving properties. For this reason, massage is the best technique for muscular disorders, menstrual and abdominal pains and circulatory disorders.

The other way that oils affect us occurs when we inhale the oil. The oil enters the nose and moves to the lining of the lungs and is then absorbed into the bloodstream. When inhaled, particularly with steam inhalation, the oils' absorption into the bloodstream is much faster. This technique is the preferred method of treating any respiratory, bacterial or viral ailments.

Woman with flower and perfume bottle,
Grecian vase (c. 5th century BC) ▶

Aroma and the senses

Our sense of smell is a highly complex, fascinating and not completely understood ability. Why a particular smell triggers a memory of an event many years past, why we associate a particular smell with a happy or unhappy occurrence, or why we consider different aromas to be pleasant or unpleasant is unique to each individual.

While there are generally agreed 'nasty' smells such as those of curdled milk, rotting fish or blocked drains, there are also generally agreed 'nice' smells, such as freshly brewed coffee, newly mown grass and the fresh, ozone smell of the sea. There is also the middle ground – the smells upon which we differ. One person may find the smell of geranium essential oil delightful, while another may object to it. This objection may purely be that they dislike the smell, or that it triggers an unwanted physical reaction. For example, they may claim that it gives them a headache. This reaction has to be considered when selecting the oils. Despite the therapeutic benefits of the oils, if you dislike the smell they will be of little value to you. It may well be the case – but it has yet to be proved – that if you dislike a smell it is not good for your body.

Further research is required to determine exactly how the mysterious, magical oils affect our emotions, but what is known is that the area of the brain which governs smell is linked with the part of the brain that deals with emotional responses, memory, libido and intuition. Smelling an essential oil triggers off a 'memory' or reaction which releases an emotion. The tangy, 'alive' smell of a lemon wakes us up while lavender smells fresh and cleansing. All these emotions are triggered by the effect the aroma of the oil has on the hormonal and autonomic nervous systems which control heart rate, memory and emotions.

Each different oil comes with the ability to impart its own unique effect on the emotions. Some tranquillize and calm, some uplift, enliven or clear the brain. Others are reputed to impart sensual aphrodisiac-like effects, probably by stimulating or suppressing certain hormones. So potent are these oils that their effect generally lasts about 12 hours.

The Shrine, John William Waterhouse (1849–1917)

Buying and storing oils

If you are new to the art of aromatherapy you may find the vast range of oils confusing and feel intimidated about which to buy. There are no rules – just buy an oil you like the smell of and check that it is suitable for you (see Warning page 39). Visiting a fully trained aromatherapist will provide an exciting insight into how they use the oils and they may well recommend two or three blends for you to use at home.

Always buy the best quality oils from a noted manufacturer to ensure that the method of extraction has been carried out well and the quality of the harvest which produced the plant was good. This means that the best oils will be the most expensive, but a little goes a very long way.

Essential oils are volatile substances and require care to ensure that their active properties remain active. The undiluted oils are easily corrupted by light (which is why they are stored in dark glass bottles), temperature extremes and exposure to air. Therefore, always buy your oils in small quantities and store them, tightly capped, in a cool dark cupboard.

Stored correctly and unopened, the oils will last for many years, some such as patchouli even becoming more potent with age. However, citrus-based oils such as orange, lemon and lime have a shorter shelf-life. Once you start using the oils they become exposed to the air each time you remove the cap but, with careful usage, the oils will remain at their peak for about a year.

Once the oil has been diluted in a carrier oil the shelf-life reduces considerably. It is therefore advisable to dilute only what you are going to use within the next 2–4 months.

The Soul of the Rose, John William Waterhouse (1849–1917)

Blending oils

There are over 400 oils but a skilled aromatherapist will probably use only 40, blending and mixing to achieve the desired results. This skill takes many years to learn and an aromatherapist will know which oil to substitute for another if the desired effect is not achieved.

When using oils at home you will probably have fewer available. However, try experimenting with them, using different oils and in different combinations until you achieve the desired effects. Don't try blending more than three oils at a time as you may find that you 'confuse' the oils and negate their therapeutic benefits.

When using oils for massage they need to be diluted in a carrier oil. This can be any odourless vegetable oil, but those such as almond, apricot kernel, peach or grapeseed oils are preferable as these are rich in vitamins A, D and E which are fat-soluble and so more easily absorbed by the skin. Some oils such as coconut, walnut, sesame and olive have their own unique aromas and their own therapeutic properties and, provided these are sympathetic to your essential oil, they can be used successfully.

Use a dropper as this will enable you to count the number of drops more easily – but use a clean dropper for each oil in order to avoid cross-contamination between oils.

For a body massage, 2–3 drops of essential oil should be diluted into 5ml/1tsp of base carrier oil. This should be sufficient for one massage – you do not need to be lavish with the oil. If you are using a mix of essential oils the proportion of drops to the 5ml/1tsp of carrier oil should be maintained.

WARNING

ALWAYS USE ESSENTIAL OILS WITH CARE. THERE ARE VERY FEW OILS THAT CAN BE USED IN THEIR UNDILUTED FORM SO ALWAYS DILUTE THEM UNLESS THERE IS A SPECIFIC INSTRUCTION TO USE THEM IN THEIR NEAT FORM.

BEFORE USING AN OIL, ALWAYS CHECK THAT IT IS SAFE FOR YOU. IF YOU HAVE A PRE-EXISTING MEDICAL CONDITION, ARE RECEIVING MEDICAL TREATMENT, TAKING HOMOEOPATHIC REMEDIES, ARE PREGNANT OR BREASTFEEDING, OR HAVE SENSITIVE SKIN OR A SKIN CONDITION, DO NOT USE THE OILS UNTIL YOU HAVE CHECKED WITH YOUR MEDICAL ADVISER AND A FULLY TRAINED AROMATHERAPIST.

ALWAYS CARRY OUT A PATCH TEST FIRST TO CHECK THAT YOUR SKIN WILL NOT REACT ADVERSELY TO THE OIL. DO THIS BY PLACING A DILUTED DROP ON THE SKIN. LEAVE ON FOR 24 HOURS. IF YOU SEE ANY ADVERSE REACTION SUCH AS REDDENING, SCALING OR ANY OTHER DISTURBANCE OF THE SKIN TEXTURE DO NOT USE.

The New Perfume, John William
◀ *Waterhouse (1849–1917)*

Massage and aromatherapy

Massage loosens taut muscles, soothes the skin, feels wonderful and releases a sense of well-being that can be almost spiritual. This, combined with the benefits of the magical aromas of the essential oils, provides a whole body experience that lasts for many hours.

Massage is an essential part of aromatherapy, inducing relaxation of both mind and body and also acting therapeutically to treat all manner of minor ailments. While aromatherapists vary in their use of massage techniques, their common aim is to combine two potent forces – the power of touch and the power of the essential oils which they massage into the skin.

When giving a massage you should keep this in the forefront of your mind. Your aim as a masseur should be to harness your own powers of touch in order to provide a form of non-verbal communication which carries with it the emotions you wish to transmit to the person who is receiving the massage.

Massage is very intuitive. You must try to sense through your fingertips the areas which need help. As you use different movements and pressures your partner will react in different ways, guiding you as to what feels good, what feels uncomfortable and what seems to be 'doing the trick'.

The Turkish Bath, Jean-Auguste Dominique Ingres (1780–1867)

Beginning a massage

The environment for the massage is important. Try to make it relaxing, dimming the lights and perhaps playing some soothing music. For a romantic, sensual massage you may want to light an aromatherapy burner or some scented candles to provide an amorous setting.

Make sure your partner is comfortable and lying on his or her stomach and that he or she is warm and calm. You can do the massage either standing or kneeling over him or her. Pour a few drops of the diluted oil into the palm of your hand and rub the hands gently together. Put your hands on the middle of the back and gently work outwards, spreading the oil over the whole surface of the back. You do not need to use much oil – the back should not be dripping with lotion but should have merely a sheen of oil visible.

The largest area of easily accessible skin on the body is the back and this is where most massages start. The back is also one of the vulnerable parts of the body, frequently put under strain and subject to stress-related muscle tensing, particularly around the shoulders and lower neck. Work gently on these areas, perhaps coming back to them later as your partner begins to unwind and release these pent-up muscles.

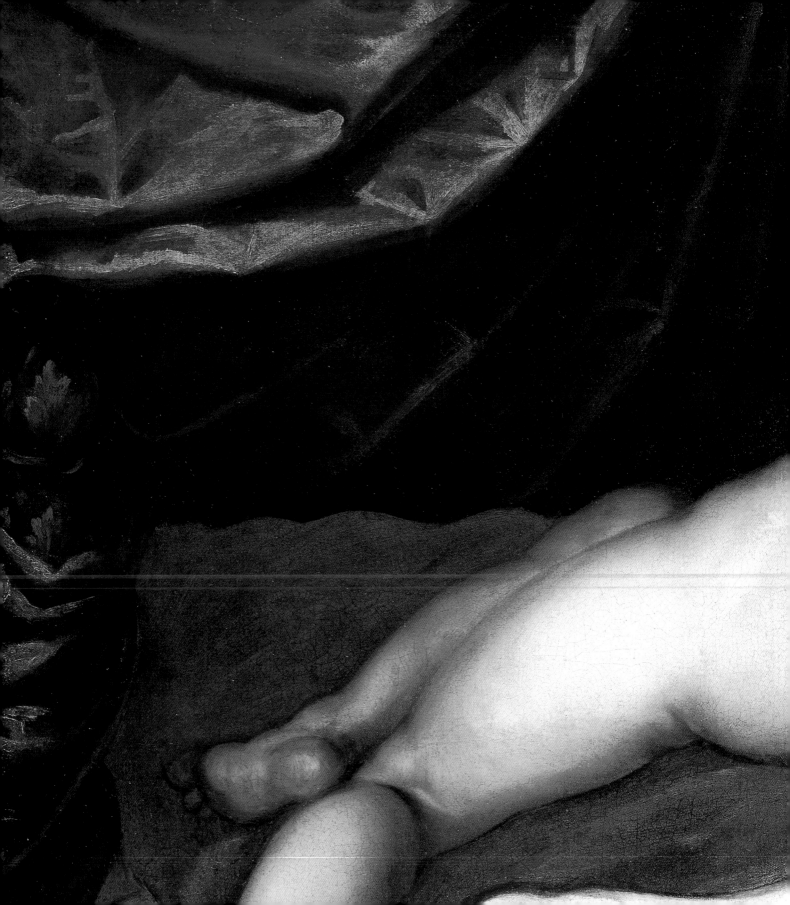

Techniques

Make long, stroking movements which are firm but not too firm. Using a circular movement, work out from the centre of the back, moving up the spine and around the shoulders, coming back down to the base of the spine. Do this gentle back rub several times to help relax your partner, keeping the movements continuous, fluid and at a slow, regular pace. This movement is based on effleurage, a stroking technique used by trained masseurs. If at any point during the massage your partner indicates that a certain area is tender or sore to the touch, stop working in that area.

You can now move on to another part of the body. Aromatherapists generally start at the base of the neck, so this would be a good place to try. Very gently massage the base of the skull, working with light movements to release any tension. Use your fingertips and thumbs to work up through the hair, as if you were washing it.

Where you move next is up to you. Trained masseurs use a combination of movements and pressures and work over the whole body with the aim of draining the lymph system of any toxins or 'stress crystals' that can build up in the body. Masseurs often finish a sequence of moves by stroking off the body in a sweeping movement, flicking the fingers away from the body to dispel any negative forces. The pressures they use vary from gentle to more forceful – but never painful.

The different pressures masseurs use include kneading the muscles (petrissage), making tapping movements (percussion) or using friction to deep rub in a circular movement. Using combinations of these movements will help get the blood flowing, improve the circulation and distribute the therapeutic properties of the oils throughout the body.

However, unless you have been on a massage course to learn these techniques, you will have to restrict yourself to giving an enjoyable, sensuous body stroking and body pressure massage, combining these movements in whatever form pleases.

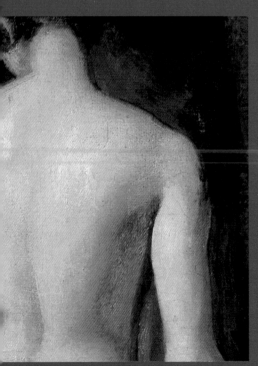

Previous pages: Mars and Venus,
Giovane Palma (1554–1628)

The Bath, William Etty (1787–1849) ▶

Inhalation and vaporization

This is the ideal method for treating any respiratory disorders. Although you can buy vaporizers, the same effect is achieved by making a steam tent. Put a few drops of the oil of your choice – for respiratory conditions try eucalyptus, marjoram, rosemary or pine – into a bowl of very hot, steaming water. Bend over the bowl and pull a towel over both your head and the bowl to capture the steam beneath the tent. Inhale the steamy droplets, and as your sinuses and airways begin to clear, you will be able to inhale bigger draughts of the scented water so that the powerful antiseptic properties of the oils can really get to work.

Burners

This is the ideal way to fragrance a room. You can use burners to create different atmospheres conducive to romance, relaxation, tranquillity or study. They can also be used to mask unpleasant cooking smells which may travel through the house, to waft antiseptic through a sickroom or to repel insects and moths.

As was the case in ancient times, most burners today have a bowl or dipped area fixed above a candle. Fill the bowl with water and then add 2–3 drops of the essential oil of your choice, depending on the mood you wish to create. For a romantic evening you could try any of the aphrodisiac oils such as neroli, ylang ylang, sandalwood, patchouli, rose, ginger, clary sage or black pepper.

The same principle of burning can be used by putting a drop or two on a light bulb or placing a bowl of scented water on a radiator.

Bathing

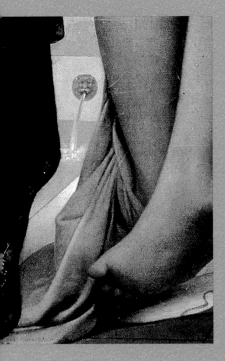

There is nothing quite like a leisurely, hot, fragranced bath for improving the mind, body and spirit. As you lie back and experience the exquisite aromas you have used to perfume the water you can let your mind go, releasing yourself from everyday cares, and revel in the experience of warm water gently caressing you and easing away aches, pains and tense muscles while your worries and concerns just float away.

Bath-time is one of the few moments we have to ourselves, so let your time in the bath be whatever you want it to be. Choose an oil because of its beautiful smell or because of its therapeutic or mood-improving qualities. Dim the lights, play some soothing music and light some candles to which you have added a drop or two of essential oil.

After your bath, massage a diluted oil all over your body, choosing the same fragrance or one complementary to the scent you used in the bathwater. A delightful night's sleep is sure to follow.

If you take your bath in the morning you will need a different, more stimulating oil so choose ones that make both the mind and the body more alert and raring to go. Try basil, peppermint, pine, cypress, juniper, rosewood or any of the zesty citrus oils such as grapefruit, bergamot, orange or lemon.

Previous pages: Odalisque, Leon Benouville
(1821–1859)

The Bather, Jean Auguste
Dominique Ingres (1780–1867) ▶

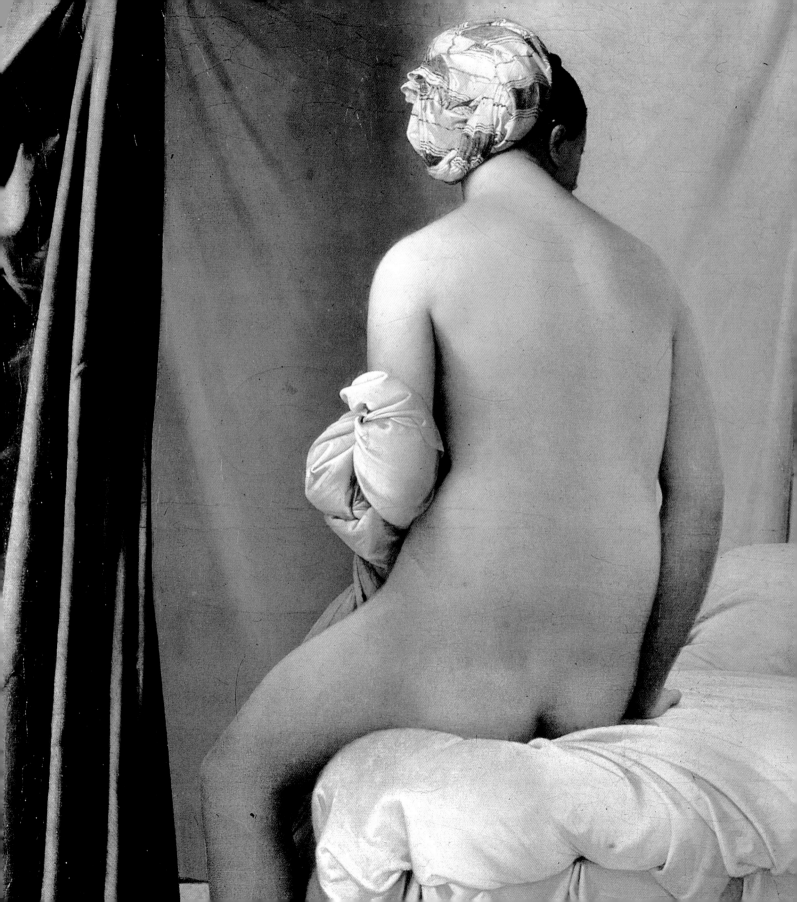

Essential Oils Directory

The art of aromatherapy harnesses the therapeutic properties of a wide range of essential oils to promote or restore a holistic sense of well-being. To do this, it is necessary to know what the different oils' extraordinary qualities are and to choose them to suit your mental, emotional and physical states.

The oils featured in the directory each have their specific powers and properties described to help you choose an oil to suit your needs. If you wish to blend oils, consider how the oils will harmonize with each other by checking their properties in the directory.

Day Dream, Dante Gabriel Rossetti (1828–1882) ▶

And the woodbine spices are wafted abroad
And the musk of the rose is blown.

(Maud, Tennyson)

He would taste the spicy wreaths
Of incense, breath'd aloft from sacred hills.

(Hyperion, Keats)

Rosewood
Aniba rosaeodora

The rosewood tree has long been valued for its beautiful wood, often made into elegant furniture and noted for its rich, amber colour. The essential oil is obtained by steam distillation of the wood chippings.

Rosewood has the ability to clear the head and steady the nerves – ideal if taking exams or making work presentations. Its relaxing and uplifting properties can help overcome emotional crises and feelings of depression. It has a mild analgesic effect and so may help with headaches and nausea. It also has a deodorant effect and can be used on sweaty feet.

Rosewood is not a widely used oil, probably because it has received little research to identify its wider properties, and also because it is being extensively felled in the South American rainforests, with subsequent environmental damage. Try to buy supplies made from environmentally controlled sources.

Roman Camomile
Anthemis nobilis

Camomile was considered a sacred herb by the ancient Egyptians, who dedicated it to their gods. Today, it is widely appreciated for its culinary, medicinal and therapeutic uses.

Its anti-inflammatory and calming properties can be used to soothe dry skin or ease rheumatic pains. Use it to ease skin problems such as eczema, dermatitis and acne and reduce the pain of sprained or swollen joints.

With its strong, herbaceous aroma, camomile also has the ability to calm the nerves and ease the problems generated by stress. It can be used before bedtime to promote restful sleep by relieving nervous tension and banishing nightmares.

Often used to treat menopausal problems, camomile can help reduce hot flushes, sweating and fluid retention. It can also help ease menstrual problems such as painful periods, premenstrual tension and irregular periods. Add 3 drops to a hot compress and apply to the abdominal area to help relieve cramps, stomach ache or lower back pain.

Its antiseptic properties can help reduce the irritation of conjunctivitis. Put 2 drops in a bowl of warm water and use a cotton pad to wipe the area (never put undiluted oils on the eye).

Until the day breaks and the shadows flee
away, I will get me to the
mountain of myrrh and to the hill
of frankincense.

(The Song of Solomon)

Here's flowers for you;
Hot lavender, mints, savory, marjoram;
The marigold, that goes to bed wi' the sun,
And with him rises weeping.

(The Winter's Tale, Shakespeare)

Frankincense
Boswellia carterii

The three wise kings arrived at Bethlehem bearing gifts to honour the newborn baby Jesus and one of the gifts was the rare and precious oil of frankincense, a sweet-smelling resin from Arabia.

Effective at both relaxing and rejuvenating at the same time, frankincense is known to lift the spirits and so is used in the treatment of stress and depression. It has also been found to be effective in boosting the immune system and can help in the treatment of a variety of skin problems and cystitis.

Use 2–3 drops in a relaxing bath at night to promote calmness and peace of mind. During times of depression and sadness, place a drop on a hanky and inhale the uplifting scent until your mood changes.

For ageing skin or to assist in the healing of minor wounds, massage or apply the diluted oil to the affected part. Add to the bathwater to help relieve the discomfort of cystitis.

When suffering from colds and flu, use 2–3 drops of frankincense in a burner in the sickroom to help immune system recovery. This aromatic oil will also create a warm, cosy atmosphere – which is another reason why it is often used at Christmas.

Marigold
Calendula officinalis

Often referred to by its botanical name of calendula, marigold has been used for thousands of years as a skin healer and it is ideal for treating and soothing a number of skin conditions.

In the Middle Ages marigold was thought to symbolize jealousy. Later on, in the 19th century, the Shaker religious sect believed marigold to be an effective cure for gangrene because of its strong antibacterial and antiseptic properties.

When applied diluted onto the skin, marigold has a toning, anti-inflammatory and healing effect and can help speed up the healing process of wounds and cuts as well as minor burns and scalds. Marigold is ideal for the treatment of fungal skin complaints such as athlete's foot – its pungent aroma helps mask the odour of sweaty feet while its antiseptic properties get to work on the cause.

It is also advised for treating greasy skin and can help with eczema and psoriasis. In addition, chilblains and bruises can be eased greatly by applying marigold.

Ylang ylang
Cananga odorata var. genuina

The aphrodisiac qualities of ylang ylang have long been celebrated by the Indonesians, who still strew its petals on the marriage bed of newly married couples.

Ylang ylang has a spicy, exotic and mysterious aroma which uplifts and relaxes. It is often used to overcome impotence or frigidity but can also be used by those suffering from frustration, anxiety, depression and other stress-related disorders. It is also said to help combat insomnia.

The Victorians added the ylang ylang oil to Macassar hair oil to help stimulate the scalp and encourage hair growth, and today aromatherapists still recommend it for this use. It can also be used as a hair rinse by putting two drops in the rinsing water or as a general skin tonic or treatment for oily skin.

Ylang ylang has long been acknowledged by the Chinese as a circulatory and heart balancer. It can be used to help overcome palpitations and slow down the rate of breathing and to reduce high blood pressure.

This oil should be used in small quantities as it can cause headaches or nausea if you overdose or use it too frequently.

Camphor
Cinnamomum camphora

Peasants used to hang lumps of camphor around their necks in the belief that it would ward off infectious diseases – and it is easy to see why: camphor has a powerful and very distinct 'medicinal' smell.

It is a pungent oil, often used to mask other smells, and is used widely in the manufacture of toiletries and cleaning products to impart a 'hospital clean' aroma to soaps, detergents and disinfectants.

There are three types of camphor: white, brown and yellow. Only the white camphor is used for aromatherapy as the other two are irritant, toxic and carcinogenic. This fact should alert you to treat camphor oil with caution.

Although it is very effective at treating acne and oily and inflamed skin, do not use it until you have carried out a patch test to check for sensitivity. It is also used to boost the circulation and treat muscular and joint pains such as arthritis, rheumatism and sprains.

As the peasants did, you too can use it to treat or ward off respiratory infections such as bronchitis, coughs, chills, colds and flu but, rather than applying it to the skin, add a drop or two to a burner and place in the sickroom.

Camphor is perhaps best used as an insect deterrent. Flies, moths and other winged creatures find its smell overwhelming and prefer to be elsewhere.

*The odors of ointments are more durable
than those of flowers.*

(*Essays of Praise*, Bacon)

Neroli
Citrus aurantium var. amara

Named after the 17th-century princess from Nerola
who introduced this oil to Italian society, neroli is also
known as orange blossom and is produced from the
delicate, fragrant flowers of the orange tree.

Neroli became a 'signature' perfume of the
prostitutes of Madrid, whose clients were thus able to
easily identify them, but the flower blossoms also have
a more romantic association: they have long been used
in various folk cultures in bridal bouquets and garlands
to symbolize purity and virginity and help calm the
happy couple's nerves on their wedding night.

Today it is also highly valued for its ability to calm the
emotions, promote confidence and relieve agitation,
anxiety and stress. Sensual, relaxing and spiritual, neroli
makes a superb massage oil to promote harmony
in the bedroom. It can also calm those who are
experiencing intense emotional distress or fright and is
often advised for 'first night' nerves, stage fright, when
speaking in public or attending an interview.

When massaged onto the skin it helps to reduce
stretch marks, thread veins and scars and tones the
complexion of sensitive, mature or wrinkled skin.
Because of its ability to boost a sluggish circulation,
neroli can energize and help overcome palpitations. It is
also recommended for digestive complaints such as
diarrhoea, indigestion and colic.

Bergamot
Citrus bergamia

Whenever you feel a little insecure, put a drop of
bergamot on a handkerchief and sniff its confidence-
building properties, for bergamot has the ability to lift
the spirits and invigorate. Its light, citrus aroma
refreshes and is ideal for using in a burner to eliminate
unpleasant musty smells in rooms or to reduce the
odour of cooking.

Bergamot is used to impart the distinctive flavour
found within Earl Grey tea, so make a cup whenever
you feel you need to be a bit more alert. The oil also
has the ability to settle the digestive system and
promote appetite and can be inhaled or massaged into
the skin to promote these properties.

When it is used on the skin, bergamot's antiseptic
properties will help combat spots and other skin
problems. It also has antiviral properties and so can be
used to treat cold sores by dabbing the diluted oil on
the affected part, while its analgesic ability will help
combat muscle aches and pains.

Although bergamot can be very helpful in treating
stress-related skin conditions such as eczema and
psoriasis, some may experience unwanted sensitivity, so
carry out a patch test first to see if your skin is suited
to using bergamot.

Avoid sunbathing if you have applied bergamot to the
skin as it can cause pigmentation changes.

Know you the land where the lemon trees bloom? In the dark foliage the gold oranges glow.

(Wilhelm Meisters Lehrjahre, Goethe)

Lemon
Citrus limonum

Although lemon had been used in ancient times to repel insects and perfume clothes, its fame did not spread until many centuries later when the British navy issued lemons to their sailors to help combat scurvy. As they travelled the globe, the merits of lemon became more widely appreciated, although the Spanish had long believed that their lemons were the answer to a wide range of ills.

Its astringent properties make it ideal for treating oily skin, acne and cold sores and it is said to help prevent wrinkles because of its anti-ageing properties. When combined with tea tree oil (see page 72), lemon can help treat warts and verrucae.

Lemon stimulates the circulation and can help reduce high blood pressure. It also has a detoxifying effect on the liver. When diluted in water and sprayed around a room it imparts a fresh, clean smell and deters insects. Also, its antiseptic properties will help combat airborne infections when it is used in the sickroom.

Fresh, light, cool and slightly tart, the lemon essence sharpens the mind, clarifies the intellect and helps dispel confusion.

Lemon is phototoxic so do not expose skin to the sun for at least 12 hours after applying lemon oil. It must always be diluted as lemon can cause irritation on sensitive skin. Do a patch test before using.

Grapefruit
Citrus paradisii

Grapefruit is part of the citrus family and has the same light and zingy, cooling and cleansing properties.

It can overcome all the 'heavy' emotions that can weigh you down, so whenever your spirits need a little lift, grab the grapefruit. It has the ability to dispel depression, headaches, nervous exhaustion and stress. Dab neat oil on a hankie and just inhale its uplifting properties.

Grapefruit can be massaged on before exercise to help boost the circulatory system and warm up muscles and joints. It also helps in the treatment of rheumatic pain, particularly if one of the symptoms is a sensation of heat in the joints. It can also be massaged on the areas where cellulite and water retention occur. Its astringent properties are valuable in the fight against acne or congested and oily skin.

Grapefruit has a short shelf life as it oxidizes quickly once exposed to the air. Also, do not use it on the skin if you are going out into sunshine as it is phototoxic.

Gathering Citron,
◀ *Frederick Leighton (1836–1896)*

He hangs in the shades the orange bright,
Like golden lamps in a green night . . .
And makes the hollow seas, that roar,
Proclaim the ambergris on the shore.

(*Bermudas*, Marvell)

Of wealthy lustre was the banquet room
Fill'd with pervading brilliance and perfume:
Before each lucid panel fuming stood
A censor fed with myrrh and spiced wood.

(*Lamia*, Keats)

Orange
Citrus sinensis

Natives of China, oranges are used as gifts during the Chinese New Year to symbolize happiness and prosperity. Now cultivated throughout the world, the orange is highly valued for its revitalizing effect on both the circulatory and nervous systems.

When it is massaged onto the body, orange boosts the flow of blood and helps to combat water retention and palpitations as well as toning dull and oily complexions.

While reinforcing the immune system and helping the body combat fevers, colds and flu, orange also acts very well on the digestive system to help relieve constipation and dyspepsia. Simply massaging the oil over the affected part of the body will ease the symptoms and its antispasmodic effects help reduce abdominal pain or distention, indigestion, wind, nausea and vomiting.

With its fresh, sweetly citrus aroma, orange can help impart a more positive frame of mind, helping to banish negative emotional traits, and it acts as a mild tranquillizer for anxiety and depression brought on by trying to do too much.

Do not apply if going out into sunlight. Carry out a patch test first as it may irritate sensitive skin.

Myrrh
Commiphora myrrha

Myrrh derives its name from the Arabic word *murr*, meaning 'bitter', and is made from the gum of the myrrh tree, rather than from its leaves, petals or bark.

It has a smoky, resinous and mysterious smell which has long been valued as an aromatic substance, playing an important religious and medicinal role in ancient Egypt, Greece and Rome.

Emotionally, myrrh has a calming, focusing and meditative effect and, as in Biblical times, it is often used in tandem with frankincense (see page 54) to calm the nerves and promote tranquillity.

Therapeutically, myrrh combines good antibacterial, antifungal and anti-inflammatory properties and can be used to treat a variety of complaints. Skin problems such as chapped skin, eczema and athlete's foot benefit from being massaged with myrrh and respiratory illnesses such as bronchitis, influenza, coughs and catarrh can be alleviated by steam inhalation of the oil. It can be used as a gargle for mouth and throat problems. Just add a drop or two to a glass of warm water to help provide relief from laryngitis, mouth ulcers, abscesses and sore gums.

Myrrh should be used in moderation. Pregnant women should use it with caution.

Cypress
Cupressus sempervirens

As aromatic plants bestow
No spicy fragrance while they grow;
But crushed or trodden to the ground,
Bestow their balmy sweets around.

(*The Captivity*, Goldsmith)

As with most of the evergreen oils, cypress has a fresh, clean, pine needle aroma, ideal for clearing a sluggish mind and promoting clear thinking as it is both refreshing and restoring.

Because of its strong astringent properties, cypress oil can be diluted and used to care for oily or spotty skin. If you suffer from sweaty feet, massage in a little diluted cypress oil and allow its antiperspirant properties to get to work.

It is very good for easing joint pains such as those experienced with arthritis and it can alleviate menstrual cramps; massage it over the area causing pain or discomfort. It stimulates the circulation and so can help those suffering from varicose veins, thread veins and piles. It can be used to ease coughs when inhaled over a steam bath.

Cypress is often advised for those suffering grief or loss as it is very comforting.

Botanical illustration of cypress

Eucalyptus
Eucalyptus globulus

The eucalyptus gum tree was thought to cleanse the environment, so the frail and sickly often moved to areas where the tree grew, in the hope that their health would improve. It is noted for its powerful antiseptic properties and it is easy to see why such faith was put in the pungent eucalyptus.

The leaves and older branches of the tree produce a pale yellow oil with the ability to purify the air and act as an insect repellent.

Its sweet, menthol fragrance is used to treat respiratory infections and it is ideal when added to a steam inhalation for clearing a blocked nose and the other congestive sinus symptoms of a cold. It is also used to bring down fever and reduce the effects of a cough, sore throat or bronchitis. It may also help clear the airways of asthmatics.

Burning eucalyptus oil in the sickroom will help purify the air. Massaging the oil on the chest will help clear the airways, making breathing easier and so allowing cold and flu sufferers to sleep more easily.

Eucalyptus also has diuretic properties and can be used to treat cystitis. It is a detoxifying oil and can help alleviate the symptoms of arthritis.

As eucalyptus acts as an antidote to homeopathic remedies you should avoid using the oil if you are taking any such medications.

Diabetics should avoid using this oil.

Botanical illustration of eucalyptus

Fennel
Foeniculum vulgare

The ancient Greeks believed fennel provided courage and strength and their athletes consumed it in the hope that it would improve their performances at the games, while in the Middle Ages it was thought to ward off witches.

With its sweet, aniseed-smelling aroma, fennel is valued for its calminative effect. It is very good for the digestion and gives relief from nausea, indigestion and wind. It is also thought to suppress the appetite and so is recommended for those who are overweight.

It is often advised for treating cellulite as it is thought to help remove toxins from the body and has a stimulating effect on the circulation. Massage fennel over the 'orange peel' areas such as the thighs, hips and abdomen to help get rid of the unsightly cellulite.

Fennel is thought to have a beneficial effect on the menstrual cycle and is often used to regularize periods, help overcome cramps and combat water retention. It can also be used as a mouthwash if you have a gum infection.

Fennel should not be used by pregnant or breast-feeding women or those who have epilepsy. Don't use if your skin is very sensitive.

Hyssop
Hyssopus officinalis

But flowers distill'd though
they with winter meet,
Leese but their show; their
substance still lives sweet.

(Sonnet V, Shakespeare)

The Ancient Greeks used hyssop to purify sacred places or to strew upon the floor and sweeten the air, while the Romans used it to protect against the plague. Today hyssop's warm and toning effect is employed to encourage spiritual awareness, alertness and clear thinking.

When used in a full body massage, hyssop can boost the circulation and its warming properties help in the treatment of muscular and joint pains. It is reputed to help remove uric acid in the system which aggravates rheumatic conditions and can be used externally for bruises and sores. Hyssop can be used on broken skin but only if the skin is not sensitive and the oil is diluted. When massaged over the abdominal area it can be used to help overcome appetite loss, poor digestion and bloating.

When inhaled, either by dabbing a couple of drops on a handkerchief or using in a burner, it can relieve the symptoms of asthma, breathlessness, bronchitis and other throat and chest congestion problems. It can also help ward off infection in the home.

Once believed capable of providing protection from negative influences and evil spirits, hyssop is now often used to combat negative emotional and physical symptoms such as melancholy, anxiety, fatigue, tension and stress, and to help those who easily absorb negative atmospheres and emotions created by others.

It should be used sparingly: 3–4 drops is sufficient for a whole body massage. It should not be used by those who are pregnant or are suffering from epilepsy or high blood pressure.

Botanical illustration of hyssop

◀ *Botanical illustration of fennel*

The barge she sat in, like a burnished throne,
Burn'd on the water; the poop was beaten gold
Purple the sails, and so perfumed, that
The winds were lovesick with them;

(*Anthony and Cleopatra*, Shakespeare)

Jasmine
Jasminum officinale

The delightfully fragrant jasmine's delicate star-shaped flowers yield the essential oil which captures its exotic and heady floral aroma.

Folklore tradition has always attributed jasmine with being warming to the womb and it was used to help during labour and birth. Modern-day aromatherapists still advise its use during labour and also to treat menstrual and other uterine problems as well as frigidity – its sensual properties have led to it being considered an aphrodisiac. It can be used by men to help overcome impotence by alleviating anxiety.

It has a mild analgesic action and good antiseptic properties and so can be used to overcome muscular pains and spasms, and respiratory disorders such as catarrh, coughs and laryngitis. For skin care it can be made into a lotion and applied to spots and other skin blemishes caused by dry, greasy, irritated or sensitive skin. Sometimes it can cause an adverse reaction so always carry out a patch test first.

Emotionally, jasmine is very uplifting, encouraging optimism and self-confidence. It is also very warming and relaxing and can help ease apathy, depression, anxiety and stress-related problems.

Jasmine is an expensive oil because very many blossom heads are required to extract the oil. Also, it must be picked at night when its aroma is at its most powerful.

Do not use jasmine during the first three months of pregnancy. Do not use at all if you have previously suffered a miscarriage. Use in small amounts as it can cause headaches if over-liberally applied.

Juniper
Juniperus communis

The pine-fresh aroma of juniper has long been valued for its antiseptic properties. The ancient Greeks used it to fight epidemics and during the Middle Ages the noted herbalist and physician Abbess Hildegarde von Bingen recommended hot baths of crushed juniper berries to treat respiratory infections.

Juniper stimulates and boosts the circulation, helping to warm cold hands and feet, and reduces the toxins in the body, helping to combat cellulite. It also boosts the immune system and so can help fight colds, flu and other infections.

It can help treat common skin conditions such as acne, dermatitis, eczema and oily complexions and can be used as a skin toner or, in a very diluted form, to cleanse wounds.

Juniper berries are used in laxative and diuretic preparations and it is thought that massaging the oil gently on the abdominal area will have the same effect.

Juniper helps enhance the appetite, which is why a gin-based drink (juniper berries are a key ingredient of gin) is often served an aperitif.

As juniper stimulates the uterine muscles it should not be used by pregnant women. It should also be avoided by those with kidney problems.

Jasmine design, William Morris (1834–1896)

And still she slept in azure lidded sleep,
In blanched linen, smooth, and lavender'd.

(*La Belle Dame sans Merci,* Keats)

The dried up violets and dried lavender
Still sweet, may comfort her,

(*Passing and Glassing,* Rossetti)

Cedarwood
Juniperus virginiana

Cedarwood was an important oil for the Ancient Egyptians, who used it during the mummification process. Because of its ability to repel insects, particularly moths, cedarwood chests were often used to store clothes. To preserve clothes packed away for the season, sprinkle cedarwood oil on drawer sachets and place them with clothes.

This oil has a warm, woody aroma which sweetly fragrances a room if 2–3 drops are used in a burner.

Cedarwood is an astringent oil and can be used diluted in water to clean and treat oily or blemished skin. Massage onto any areas of the body where cellulite is a problem.

Medicinally, cedarwood can be used to decongest the lungs and functions as an expectorant to relieve mucus congestion. Emotionally, it can help calm anxiety and banish fear.

Avoid cedarwood if you have high blood pressure or heart problems.

Lavender
Lavandula officinalis

The volatile oil of lavender has long been used for its soothing, healing and antiseptic properties. It can be used diluted, but it is one of the few oils that can also be used in its neat form – and often is.

It can act as a calming tonic for the nervous system, gently easing away stresses and strains. It can also help reduce nervous anxiety, exhaustion and depression. The swelling from joint strains and sprains are reduced by either bathing the area in lavender-scented water or applying 1–2 drops of neat essential oil and massaging it into the affected area.

Headaches and migraines benefit from lavender. Massage 2 drops onto the temples or affected part. When taken internally, it can help to soothe flatulence and colic. Take an infusion 3 times a day before or after meals.

Lavender's strong antiseptic and antibacterial properties can be used to treat minor cuts and burns, skin infections such as athlete's foot and skin conditions such as dermatitis and eczema – simply dab the oil on the affected part using a few drops of oil on a cotton wool pad.

Put a few sprigs of lavender or 2–3 drops of lavender essential oil in a drawer sachet and keep it with your clothes to give them a fresh, meadow-sweet smell.

Botanical illustration of Lavender

Girl Selling Lavender, W. M. Craig (1788–1828) ▶

Tea tree
Melaleuca alternifolia

When Captain Cook landed at Botany Bay in 1770, his men discovered the tea tree and made its sticky leaves into a spicy drink, thus rediscovering the ancient aborigine herbal remedy which had been used to treat all manner of ills.

Tea tree has a strong, antiseptic aroma with excellent antiseptic and antifungal properties. An Australian analysis carried out in 1923 discovered tea tree to be 12 times stronger than carbolic acid when used as an antiseptic bactericide. Because of this, it is ideal for using in a vaporizer to kill germs in the sickroom or to combat colds, flu, fever and infectious illnesses such as chickenpox. Inhaling tea tree can help alleviate asthma and other respiratory conditions.

Dab it on in neat form to treat acne and cold sores on the face, or rub on the feet to combat athlete's foot. Make it into a rinse to help combat dandruff or use it to clean abscesses, blisters, minor burns and insect bites or to clean pus from wounds.

While tea tree is non-toxic and non-irritant, always carry out a patch test first to check for sensitivity as it can irritate some skins.

Botanical illustration of melissa

Melissa
Melissa officinalis

Also known as lemon balm, melissa is one of the oldest medicinal herbs. It was – and still is – a popular plant in many cottage gardens, where it will attract bees. This feature led the Greeks to give it the name melittena, meaning honey bee.

Melissa was identified as the elixir of life by Paracelsus, the 16th-century Swiss alchemist, and it is still considered by some to confer longevity.

Medicinally, it is best known for its effect on allergies. When used in small quantities it can help skin conditions such as eczema, and it has also been noted for its success in treating allergic asthma. It also helps calm and regulate the menstrual cycle and is said to help lower blood pressure by calming over-fast breathing and slowing down the heartbeat.

Melissa's fresh citrus-like smell works on the emotions to soothe, calm and uplift, dispelling negative or distressing thoughts. It works well for those suffering depression, particularly after experiencing a bereavement. It is also a 'happy' oil, according to the 11th-century Persian physician Avicenna, who claimed that it 'maketh the heart merry and joyful and strengtheneth the vital spirits'.

In a very diluted form use melissa in the bath or on the skin, or use in a burner to refresh the room and impart a happy atmosphere.

Try to buy unadulterated melissa, as it is frequently sold diluted with lemon, lemon grass, verbena or citronella.

Always use in small quantities, particularly if you have sensitive skin. Do not use during pregnancy or before going out into the sun as it may cause irritation.

Peppermint
Mentha piperita

Refreshing and cooling, uplifting and restoring, peppermint is one of the most useful – and popular – oils.

Peppermint is believed to provide inspiration and insight because it acts as a stimulant and awakens the brain. For this reason it can be used during creative work, study or exams to pep up the brain cells.

It is frequently used to flavour food or sweets because of its ability to settle the digestive system. The essential oil is thought to stimulate energy in the stomach and intestines and is used to treat various digestive problems including colic, irritable bowel syndrome and nausea. Massage the peppermint oil over the stomach areas or inhale from the bottle to combat symptoms. It is also excellent at overcoming travel sickness, so put a drop on a handkerchief and inhale.

Peppermint also has an anti-infectious action and can be used to treat colds and flu where there is headache, fever and sore throat. When used in a steam inhalation bowl, peppermint can help ease asthma attacks and bronchitis. It also has expectorant properties and can help to alleviate congested sinuses.

Peppermint's antiseptic properties and ability to cool the skin make it an ideal application for treating tired feet. Massage the oil over the foot in gentle, pressing strokes to revitalize the feet.

Pregnant women should avoid using peppermint during pregnancy and it should be used sparingly as it may cause irritation to sensitive skins.

Basil
Ocimum basilicum

By simply crushing a basil leaf in your fingers you can release its wonderfully clean, uplifting aroma, which is fresh, pungent and reviving.

Basil is noted for its antidepressant properties as well as its ability to clear the mind and stimulate the memory. For this reason it is ideal for when your spirits need lifting and when you need to concentrate, particularly when taking exams.

Its clear, sweet smell helps 'wake up' the system and so a few drops added to a morning bath will help you start your day off with more alertness than usual. For the same reason use it also when you feel fatigue creeping up. When combined with any of the citrus oils, its reviving properties are further enhanced and so it is ideal for treating jet lag.

Basil is also noted for its medicinal properties. It can help treat migraines, nausea and nervous tension and is said to assist in regulating menstrual cycles. It works very well in settling the digestive system, particularly for upset stomachs and vomiting.

As well as being an antidepressant, basil also has strong antiseptic qualities and will help soothe insect bites and stings – just dab a little on with a cotton wool ball. Sprinkle a couple of drops on a hankie and inhale when you have a cold or flu. It will uplift you as well as help alleviate your symptoms.

Basil, if used in excess, can act as a depressant, so use very sparingly. It should not be used during pregnancy, and those with sensitive skins or an existing skin condition should avoid using basil on the skin.

Marjoram
Origanum majorana

Marjoram's botanical name stems from the Greek words *oros* and *ganos*, meaning 'joy of the mountains' and marjoram truly is a joy – fresh, warm and herbaceous with a slightly woody aroma.

It was much valued by the ancient Egyptians, who dedicated it to the god Osiris, the king of the afterlife and eternity, used it as a funereal herb and placed it on the graves of the dead. They also used it in making perfumes, unguents and medicines.

In herbal medicine it has been recommended as a voice preservative and drinking an infusion of honey and marjoram is said to help relieve the vocal cords.

Today, marjoram is valued for its warming, comforting and calming properties and is advised for those suffering from insomnia, grief, headaches and migraine, nervous tension and hypertension.

It has strong antispasmodic abilities and so can be used to aid respiratory problems such as asthma, bronchitis and coughs or massaged over the affected area to relieve digestive problems such as wind, constipation and indigestion. It is also very useful for treating menstrual problems such as PMS and absent or painful and cramping periods.

When it is massaged over tired muscles and joints or added to a relaxing bath, marjoram's warming properties bring relief.

As marjoram has a strong sedative action it should not be used to treat depression; instead, choose a more spirit-lifting oil. Marjoram should not be used during pregnancy.

Geranium
Pelargonium graveolens

Geranium is thought to balance the mind and body because of its strong ability to regulate hormonal and emotional swings.

It has a floral, spicy and exotic aroma and is sometimes used as an aphrodisiac because of its ability to provoke sensual, liberating emotions.

For the workaholic, geranium can help promote sensitivity and relaxed spontaneity after a hard day at work. It can also function as a tonic to alleviate lethargy and fatigue.

Often considered the 'women's oil', geranium can be used to alleviate menstrual and menopausal problems. It boosts the circulation, thus benefiting the skin and helping to combat acne. For the same reason it can help nerve and joint pain, particularly neuralgia and rheumatism. When massaged into the areas of the body where cellulite accumulates it can help combat unsightly 'orange peel' skin.

Geranium's powerful anti-inflammatory properties are on a par with lavender (page 70) and so it can also be successfully used to reduce the effects of gastritis, colitis, eczema, psoriasis and athlete's foot. It also acts as a diuretic.

Geranium is non-toxic, non-irritant and usually non-sensitizing, although there is the possibility of a reaction in those with hypersensitive skin or suffering from contact dermatitis.

This oil should definitely be included in your aromatherapy pharmacopoeia and it blends well with most other oils.

Pine
Pinus sylvestris

The Native Americans, who believed pine warded off lice and fleas, used the dried needles to stuff mattresses to protect against them at night. They also believed it had strong ascorbic properties and used extract of pine needles to prevent scurvy.

Emotionally, pine is very uplifting, stimulating and refreshing and when its resinous, woody aroma is inhaled it goes into battle against pessimistic thoughts and other emotional conditions that are brought on by negative thinking. Its fresh, 'alive' scent can also help overcome fatigue.

Refreshing pine can be inhaled over a steam bowl or vapourizer to combat respiratory tract problems such as catarrh, bronchitis, flu and asthma. When added to the bath or massaged over the affected area, pine can ease muscular aches and pains, particularly those associated with rheumatic conditions.

Noted for its strong antiseptic properties, pine oil is very effective in combating excessive perspiration when added to the bath.

Always carry out a patch test before using pine as some people may experience sensitivity, particularly those with allergic skin conditions.

Black Pepper
Piper nigrum

The warm, soothing effect generated by black pepper makes it ideal for treating muscle aches and pains. When applied just before you warm up for exercise it can help boost a sluggish circulatory system. It is also said to be very valuable in the treatment of chilblains.

The Indians believed pepper gave remarkable powers of physical endurance and so holy men would swallow grains of pepper every day to give them the stamina to cover the many miles they walked each day.

It has a pungent aroma and is often used to help reduce fever or act as an expectorant, so apply it to the chest when you have a cold or flu. It can also be used to help stimulate the digestive system to overcome appetite loss or nausea as well as to treat constipation, diarrhoea or flatulence.

Black pepper is reputed to have aphrodisiac qualities because of its ability to stimulate the senses and promote physical energy by combating fatigue.

Botanical illustration of pine ◄

Botanical illustration of black pepper ►

Patchouli
Pogostemon cablin

Mysterious, musky and earthy, patchouli is an exotic oil noted for its sensual, aphrodisiac qualities. Long used in the East to scent clothes and linen, it became popular in the West during the 19th century as a perfume to scent the very popular Indian fabrics and shawls that were imported in large quantities.

Today in Malaysia and Japan it is used as an antidote to snake bites, while in the West its insect-repelling properties are well known and widely used. Put a couple of drops on a candle in the bedroom to deter insects while you sleep.

It is a powerful, spicy and warm oil. Just a little will help boost the body and spirit, but if you use too much it will have the opposite effect and act as a sedative. Patchouli's ability to provide harmony of body and spirit is the reason why it is often advised for those suffering sexual anxiety, impotence or frigidity. This, combined with its antidepressive effect, further enhances its power as an aphrodisiac.

On a less romantic note, patchouli also has strong antibacterial, anti-infectious, anti-inflammatory and antifungal properties and so can be used for acne, athlete's foot, weeping eczema, oily skin and hair and to clean wounds.

Rose
Rosa damascena

To celebrate the feast of Flora, the Romans scattered rose petals amid the celebrations. They also wove garlands of roses to wear during their frequent feasts and celebrations in the hope that it would prevent them from getting too drunk.

Traditionally associated with Aphrodite, the Greek goddess of love, beauty and fertility, the fragrant rose is still used today to treat problems such as frigidity or impotence and is reputed to have aphrodisiac properties. It is also recommended for menstrual and menopausal problems because of its affinity with the reproductive system.

Ideal for treating the skin complaints such as broken veins, dry skin, eczema, cold sores and mature or wrinkled skin, rose can be massaged on the face or body to stimulate the circulation and tone the skin. When made into a lotion by diluting in distilled water, rosewater makes a very good skin toner. Add a drop of witch hazel if you have oily skin.

Rose is a sedative and can help reduce the effects of depression, shock, anger or despair to provide a sense of calmness and well-being. Use it however you like – in a massage, dropped onto a lighted candle, in a burner or vapourizer or just a few drops added to some rose petal pot pourri to fragrance the room.

It is also noted for its effect on the digestive system and can be used to treat nausea and stomach upsets.

Pregnant women should avoid using rose in the first four months of pregnancy.

The Roses of Heliogabalus,
Sir Lawrence Alma-Tadema (1836–1912)

*There's rosemary, that's for remembrance;
pray, love, remember: and there is pansies,
that's for thoughts.*

(*Hamlet*, Shakespeare)

Rosemary
Rosemarinus officinalis

Rosemary has long been considered a sacred herb in many civilizations. It was burnt at shrines by the Ancient Greeks who, together with the Romans, considered it symbolic of remembrance and loyalty. The Greeks dedicated it to Apollo, god of medicine, music, poetry and prophecy.

During the Middle Ages garlands or sprigs of rosemary were worn to bring good luck and provided protection against evil spirits, magic and witchcraft. It was also used to protect against the plague and other infectious illnesses.

Rosemary is a fresh, invigorating and herbaceous oil which stimulates and restores the senses. When rubbed over aching muscles it helps warm, revive and promote suppleness and it is a very good oil to use as an antirheumatic.

The fresh aroma that rosemary imparts helps fight fatigue and debility and revives a depressed spirit. It can renew enthusiasm and bolster self-confidence.

Rosemary can be used as a body massage to help combat fluid retention and cellulite. Use it in the rinsing water after shampooing dark hair to add sparkle to dull locks and cleanse the scalp.

It has good antibacterial and antiseptic properties and so can be used to treat colds and flu and respiratory infections. It is also said to help reduce period pains and headaches.

Before using rosemary on the skin, carry out a patch test to check for sensitivity. Do not use rosemary during pregnancy, or if you have epilepsy or high blood pressure.

Sandalwood
Santalum album

Sandalwood has had over 4000 years of continuous use and is the oldest known perfume material. Traditionally, this musky, exotic oil was used as an incense or embalming constituent and in India, where the tree is protected, it was frequently carved into religious icons, used to build temples or burned as incense to gods. The yogis used it to encourage a contemplative state and enhance their meditations. It has long been held in veneration by the Chinese, who use it as a funeral herb to anoint and embalm the dead.

Today, sandalwood is used to quell a turbulent mind and open up creative thought. It can help vanquish depression, insomnia and other stress-related conditions and can also be used to treat minor skin conditions such as spots or dry, cracked or chapped skin. It is ideal when used as an aftershave to help combat razor rash.

Sandalwood has good antibacterial and antiseptic properties and when made into a gargle it can help alleviate the symptoms of a sore, scratchy throat. It can also help reduce the symptoms of eczema, particularly when combined with juniper, camomile or lavender.

The warm, woody and sensual properties of sandalwood have also given it a reputation for acting as an aphrodisiac. Apply it as a perfume, add to the bath to create a fragrant, steamy atmosphere or simply use in a full body massage to harness its reputed powers.

Like precious odors — most fragrant when they are incensed or crushed.

(*The Captivity*, Goldsmith)

Clary sage
Salvia sclarea

The botanical name for clary sage is derived from the words 'clear', 'saving' and 'healing', capturing the essence of this very effective oil. Highly esteemed in the Middle Ages, it was called 'clear eye' by mediaeval herbalists, who prescribed it for all manner of eye complaints. Today, clary sage is often used in preference to the more common sage as it has wider curative properties, does not contain the chemical thujone (which is toxic) and has a more pleasant, nutty aroma.

Clary sage has a fresh, herby aroma and soothes and warms. It has the ability to induce a relaxing, soothing effect which in some people may induce a pleasant sensation of drowsiness, making it ideal to add to a night-time bath, particularly after a stressful day. Those sensitive to clary sage may also experience vivid dreams. However, it can also have a 'disconnecting' effect on the emotions and while it is one of the oils noted for its sensual, aphrodisiac properties, it should be used with caution as the effects may not be appropriate during everyday life.

Its antispasmodic ability makes it ideal for treating aches and pains, high blood pressure, and throat and respiratory problems, particularly asthma as it helps relax the spasms in the bronchial tubes. When massaged over the abdomen it can help relieve menstrual cramp or digestive pains.

Clary sage can prevent excessive sweating and so can help reduce the production of sebum, making it ideal for oily skins and scalps.

Do not drink alcohol when using clary sage as it can exaggerate its effect. Do not use if pregnant. Do not drive or operate machinery.

Ginger
Zingiber officinalis

Spicy, warm and pungent, ginger has been used for many centuries by the Chinese, who believed that it imparted strength and promoted long life. It was also used medicinally for a variety of complaints and as both a spice and a medicant was highly esteemed throughout the world from ancient times to the Middle Ages.

Spiritually, ginger is thought to boost will power in those lacking drive or tending towards procrastination or doubt. It is also thought to act as a sexual tonic – the women of Senegal weave the ginger root into belts to arouse their husbands.

Only the root of the ginger plant is used to extract the essential oil which today is used mainly for its ability to calm or stimulate the digestive system and is advised for poor appetite, indigestion, diarrhoea and wind as well as for nausea and travel sickness.

It also is noted for its decongesting properties so if you suffer from blocked up sinuses or bronchitis, add a couple of drops to a bowl of steaming water.and inhale to help clear the sinuses.

Ginger can also be used to 'warm up' the system when suffering from chills, colds and flu. Apply as a massage or add a few drops to a warming bath.

It has the ability to act as a stimulant on the circulatory system and when massaged onto the affected part can help warm cold hands and feet and rheumatic joints that feel cold.

Women gathering sage,
◀ *illuminated manuscript (c. 1385)*

Aromatherapy Recipes

Many of the essential oils listed in the Essential Oils
Directory (see pages 50–85) have characteristics in common
and by blending those which complement each other you can
make up very effective recipes. As we all react differently to
smell, experimentation will help you to choose and mix those
oils that work best for you.

If you do not want to use some of the suggestions here, look in the
directory and choose an oil you do like which also has the properties you
are seeking. When several oils are described for treating one symptom,
opt first for the oil you prefer. If you have more than one symptom you
wish to treat, choose an oil that fulfils both needs.

   For safety's sake you should never use more than 10 drops of any oil or
combination of oils each day. Using more provides such a clash of aromas
that you will negate any positive effects the oils have. You will also risk
aggravating your condition rather than improving it. Provided you carry
out a skin patch test on any of the oils to which you may be sensitive, you
will avoid harming your skin.

The Magdalen Reading,
Ambrosius Benson (1519–1550) ▶

Rosewater skin toner

To 50 ml/2 fl oz of spring or mineral water add 15 drops of rose. Shake well and leave for a minimum of a week in a cool, dark cupboard. During this time the oil's aroma will fragrance the water. However, the oil will not dissolve and will therefore need to be filtered. To do this, use a coffee filter paper or some kitchen paper and pour in the mix. The filtered water can then be bottled up.

Use the toner to clean the face after removing makeup or to keep the skin clear if you are prone to spots, eczema or dermatitis.

Scented drawer sachets

To keep your clothes smelling sweet and fresh, make a small cushion and stuff it with lavender sprigs. As the smell of the sprigs gradually fades, you can freshen it by adding a few drops of lavender oil. If you stuff the sachet with cotton wool you can add any oil you like.

Traditionally, clothes chests were made of cedarwood to protect the clothes from moths and insects. You can also use this oil if you are storing your clothes away for the season.

Revitalizing foot bath

After a long day on your feet, there is nothing that eases uncomfortable aches and pains quite like a footbath.

Add 6 drops of peppermint to a bowl of hot (not too hot) water, swish it around and then sit comfortably with both feet in the water. Relax or read a book while the peppermint soothes and tones. Pat the feet dry and then gently massage in a relaxing oil – you could try marigold or cypress, which are both particularly effective in combating odorous feet.

The Bath of Bathsheba,
Beham Hans Sebald (1500–1550)

Cellulite massage oil

Although the medical profession doubts the existence of cellulite, many women know that it exists. It usually manifests itself around the bottom, thighs and hips and gives the skin a crinkly, orange peel look.

Massaging the area regularly will boost the circulation and the lymphatic system, helping to get the blood flowing to the area and feeding the skin.

Make the oil by using 4 drops of fennel to 2 drops of geranium or juniper, mixed in 25 ml/1 fl oz of a carrier oil. This should be enough to last for 4–5 days.

Anti-dandruff hair tonic

After rinsing the hair of all traces of shampoo, fill the bathroom basin with clean water and add a drop of clary sage, 2 drops of rosemary and 2 drops of tea tree. Dunk your head in the water and make sure the hair is well-soaked. Squeeze out excess water and towel dry. Use this once a week.

Facial sauna

Rehydrate dry skin by making a facial infusion of water to which you have added 4 drops of lavender, 4 drops of geranium and 1 of patchouli. Swirl around and then, placing your face over the steam, make a tent over the bowl and your head with a towel. Stay in this steamy atmosphere for 5 minutes and then wipe your face with a cotton wool ball soaked in toner before applying a rich moisturiser.

A Maid Combing a Woman's Hair,
Pierre-Cécile Puvis de Chavannes (1824–1898) ▶

Cold relief inhalant

Colds and flu symptoms often make the sinuses congested. Use the same technique of making a tent steamer as for a facial toner (page 90) and add a couple of drops each of eucalyptus and tea tree.

There are many other oils which are good for colds, as explained in the Essential Oils Directory(see pages 50–85). Experiment to see which is most effective for your symptoms.

Morning wake up

Start the day off with a kick by bathing in a mix of 3 drops of basil, which will help perk up the brain, with 3 drops of lemon, cypress, neroli or bergamot, which all have a fresh, lively aroma.

Winter reviver

Whenever the weather has made you wet and miserable, make a mix of spicy and warming ginger, patchouli and frankincense to get the circulation flowing, warm up hands and feet, and impart a relaxing, warming glow to both mind and body.

Use a mix of 3 drops of ginger, 1 of patchouli and 2 of frankincense, either in a carrier lotion to apply as a warming massage, or added to the water of a long, hot bath.

Sweet dreams bath recipe

To help you unwind after a stressful day, add 4 drops each of lavender and sandalwood to the bathwater when the bath is three-quarters full. The lavender will help reduce anxiety and depression while the sandalwood will help overcome the potential of insomnia by quietening the brain.

Index

Acknowledgements

Publishing Director:
Laura Bamford

Commissioning Editor:
Jane McIntosh

Assistant Editor:
Catharine Davey

Editor:
Diana Vowles

Art Director:
Keith Martin

Senior Designer:
Ben Barrett

Picture Research:
Liz Fowler

Production Manager:
Dawn Mitchell

The publishers wish to thank the following organizations for their kind permission to reproduce the photographs in this book:

Ancient Art and Architecture Collection/Mary Jelliffe 9/Ronald Sheridan 16
AKG, London 6 (detail), 7, 28, 28/29, 60, 61 (detail), 79/Erich Lessing 34/Musee des Beaux-Arts 46/47 (detail)/Musee du Louvre 48 (detail), 49/Museo Nazionale Romano delle Terme 12, 13/Musee Vivenel/Photo: Erich Lessing 35
Bridgeman Art Library, London/Birmingham City Museums & Art Gallery 92 (detail)/Bradford Art Galleries and Museums 2, 3 (detail)/British Library, London 22/23/Christie's Images, London 38 (detail), 39 top & bottom (details)/Johnny Van Haeften Gallery, London 62 (detail)/Kunsthalle, Hamburg 63 (detail)/Lindley Library, RHS, London 77 (background)/Louvre, Paris, France/Lauros-Giraudon 40/41/Roy Miles Gallery, 29 Bruton Street, London W1 37 (detail)/Phillips, The International Fine Art Auctioneers 14/15/Piccadilly Gallery, London 55 (detail)/Victoria & Albert Museum, London 50 (detail), 51, 68/69 (background)/Walker Art Gallery, Liverpool 25 (detail)/Christopher Wood Gallery, London 36 (detail)
Christies Images 80 (detail), 81 inset, 81 (background/detail)
E.T. Archive 67/Biblioteca Estense Modena 22 left/Bibliotheque Nationale, Paris 84, 85 (background)/British Museum 20/Garrick Club 44, 45, both images are details from the painting specified in the caption/Victoria & Albert Museum 71 (detail)
Mary Evans Picture Library endpapers, 1, 27, 32/33, 66 top, 82 right, 82 left, 94
Fine Art Photographic Library Ltd 30/31 (detail)
Hulton Getty Picture Collection 96
Reed International Books Ltd./Chris Barker 65
Natural History Museum Picture Library, London 52, 53, 56, 57, 58, 59, 64, 70, 72/73, 78
The National Gallery, London, reproduced by courtesy of the Trustees 18, 19, 42/43, 86, 87, 91, all images are details from the paintings specified in the captions
Reunion des Musees Nationaux, Paris/Louvre 5, 88/89/Musee Bonna, 4 (background), all images are details from the paintings specified in the captions
Royal Botanic Gardens, Edinburgh 76 (background)
Science & Society Picture Library, Science Museum 74
Werner Forman Archive/British Museum 10

Thanks to Mr R. Starke of Chestnut Farm, Suffolk for advice regarding the distilling process.